BE STILL WITH ME

This book was created for the quiet moments.
The moments when life feels loud, when your thoughts
wander, and when you need a place to slow down
and breathe.

You don't need to rush through these pages.
There's no right pace, no pressure to finish, no expectation
to feel anything other than what you already feel.
Each page is an invitation — to pause, to reflect, to soften
your grip, and to reconnect with yourself in stillness.

As you color, let your mind rest. Let your heart open gently.
Let what needs to surface do so without judgment.

**You are safe here.
Take your time.**

YESENIA GARCIA

Books by Yesenia Garcia

Ni De Aquí, Ni De Allá
A memoir of healing, identity, and becoming.

Be Still With Me
A devotional coloring book for quiet strength and inner peace.

Copyright Disclaimer:

All rights reserved. No part of this publication, including the characters, and artwork, may be reproduced, distributed, or transmitted in any form or by any means, electronic or mechanical, without the prior written permission of the copyright owner. Unauthorized copying, reproduction, or distribution of this book is strictly prohibited.

The characters and artwork in this book are the intellectual property of the author. Any resemblance to actual persons, living or deceased, or to any existing artwork or intellectual property, is purely coincidental.

This coloring book is intended for personal use only. It is not permitted to use the content of this book for commercial purposes, such as selling or mass reproducing the artwork or activities. The purchase of this book grants the buyer the right to use it for personal enjoyment and non-commercial purposes.

Please respect the copyright of the author, as well as the intellectual property rights associated with the content of this book. Thank you for your understanding and cooperation.

©2026 | YESENIA GARCIA | All Rights Reserved

Today I release the thoughts
I keep replaying.

I release the questions
I don't have answers for.

When memories visit in the quiet,
I let my heart loosen its grip
on what isn't meant for me.

Whatever leaves, my life makes space for what is truly mine.

Today doesn't have to be perfect.
It just needs to be gentle.

I've got this.

I don't have to overanalyze every loss.

Not every disappointment is a story about my worth.

Losing isn't proof that I'm failing, it's proof that I'm living, trying, and evolving.

Taking the chance is better than wondering, "what if?"

I release the need to control every outcome.

I choose courage over comfort.

I choose becoming, not breaking.

Today, I choose a steady mind.

To soften my heart and slow my speech so I don't feel overwhelmed.

I choose grace even when
my emotions rise.

I don't have to react
to everything I feel.

Peace is a choice I can make.

I release the need to understand everything right now.

I choose rest. I choose trust.

I choose peace.

I surrender. I release control.

I release the need to understand the timing. I release the fear that comes with the unknown.

I choose faith over fear, peace over panic, and trust over attachment.

God, fix me when I'm the problem, and protect me when I'm not.

It's okay to have bad days.

I feel what I need to feel,
and then I move forward.

I am safe. I am loved. I am not alone.

Everything I'm longing for is moving toward me, not away from me.

I don't have to fight the fear.
I can feel it and still be okay.

I am a good thing. I am enough.

When I stop being afraid to lose,
I become brave enough to grow.

I don't have to rush my healing.

Growth takes time,
and I'm allowed to move slowly.

**What's meant for me won't pass me.
I can relax into what's unfolding.**

I don't have to prove my worth today. Being here is enough.

I release what I can't carry anymore.
Peace feels lighter than control.

I am allowed to outgrow
old versions of myself.

Change means I'm becoming.

I can be strong
and still choose softness.

I trust the quiet work happening inside me, even when no one else can see it.

I don't have to solve my whole life today. One gentle step is enough.

I choose peace over pressure.
Rest is productive too.

I am learning to feel
without drowning.

I can hold emotions
without becoming them.

I am allowed to take up space without shrinking to make others comfortable.

I won't place my tenderness
in hands that can't hold it gently.

I'm learning to protect
my softness with discernment.

My heart deserves safe spaces.

I am allowed to slow down without falling behind.

I am not behind in life.

I am on my own timeline, and it is unfolding exactly as it should.

I know who I am now. I release
the past without fear.

I move forward differently
with strength, clarity,
and quiet confidence.

I trust the quiet growth happening inside me. Even when it's unseen, it is preparing me.

I can let emotions rise and fall without losing myself in them.

**Even in my quietest nights,
I am still held and guided.**

The work of my hands carries intention, care, and purpose.

I step forward into who I am becoming without fear.

CONGRATULATIONS!

If you've reached this page, I hope you feel
a little lighter than when you began.

May these moments of stillness remind you that growth
doesn't have to be loud, and strength doesn't always look
like pushing forward. Sometimes it looks like resting.
Sometimes it looks like letting go.

Carry this calm with you beyond these pages — into your
days, your choices, and the quiet spaces in between.

You are becoming, even when it feels slow.
You are held, even when you feel uncertain.
And you are allowed to move forward in peace.

Thank you for spending this time here.

YESENIA GARCIA

www.ingramcontent.com/pod-product-compliance
Lightning Source LLC
LaVergne TN
LVHW070428090526
838199LV00129B/481